DON'T TURN AWAY

POEMS IN SEARCH OF SPIRITUALITY

DON'T TURN AWAY

POEMS IN SEARCH OF SPIRITUALITY

JIM TEETERS

Acknowledgements

I want to thank the Striped Water Poets of Auburn, Washington for the good work of critiquing many of the poems in this collection. Thanks to my friend Ardelle Dudley who encourages my continued writing. I am most grateful to Lana Hechtman Ayers for her editing assistance. Also, my writing DNA mostly comes from my mother, Leone M. Teeters (deceased).

TABLE OF CONTENTS

INTRODUCTION, 3

SOUL

A CHANCE OF RAIN

SACKCLOTH AND ASHES

EARTH COTTAGE

TIME

AUTHOR, 75

DON'T
TURN
AWAY

POEMS IN SEARCH
OF SPIRITUALITY

INTRODUCTION

I searched for my Self
until I was weary,

but no one, I know now
reaches the hidden knowledge
by means of effort

Then, absorbed in "Thou art This,"
I found the place of Wine

There all the jars are filled,
but no one is left to drink.*

WONDER AND DANGER

We live in a wonderful and dangerous world. This contrast
provides us both with enormous possibilities and challenges.
As inhabitants of this modern world we mingle together and
live out our daily lives in expectancy, astonishment, boredom,
or fear.

Kindness and cruelty inhabit our human souls and fully play
a part in the mix of wonder and danger. We emerge helpless
from the womb with no control over where we live or who cares
or not cares for us. From our un-chosen parents, place, and
situation we formulate our ways of acting and reacting to our
world. The wonderful and dangerous things that we encounter
urge us on into hope or despair, joy or fear, love or hate.

We experience the ecstasy and pleasure of friendship and love as well as the excruciating pain of failure and loss. We read about the horrors of genocide as well as the beauty of a Mother Theresa. We see parents and children in delightful play and also hear the despicable tales of churchmen abusing little ones. We walk trails in nature to witness God's green or desert wonders but also witness the destruction of hurricanes and earthquakes.

The poems in this collection speak mostly to the danger but also to the wonder. I lament that I miss the possibilities. The poems are hopeful too; in that they help us recognize the ways we can embrace wonder and face danger—to feel fully alive and expectant. I invite you to weep and laugh with me in these expressions of pain and joy.

* Lal Ded of Kashmir, 14th Century (?)

SOUL

Soul

After Parker Palmer

The soul
is a wild thing, tough, clever
hard to catch
you can't chase after it
or loudly call its name

You must sit quietly
under a tree and wait
      a
      long
      time
with a bowl of grapes
decanter of wine
warm bread, then
when it comes to your side to sup
you can gather up your
      wandering soul

Pastor's Laments #1, #2, and #3

I Beat Life with a Stick (a pastor's lament #1)

I beat life with a stick
a cloud of transient dust
drifts east in a pregnant breeze
settles on dreary plains

I beat life with a stick
to get the meaning out of it
the questions I raise
blow away with the answers

I beat life with a stick
until my arms get tired
I just want to lie down
let the sun warm my sick soul

I beat life with a stick
when I finish I wear it
like a threadbare garment
and shiver

Gathering Nothing (a pastors lament #2)

I'm tired of gathering nothing
I feel so stupid
stooping to pick nothing

When I come home
my basket is empty
"What are you gathering?" my wife asks
"Nothing," I say
"Nothing again?"

"Nothing," I say
I've gathered nothing

        again

We have nowhere to go (a pastor's lament #3)

We have nowhere to go and I am the perfect one to
      lead us there.

Backstage

I would be
all I wish to be
if it weren't for
the stagehand's hook
that pulls me back
the curtains that won't open
and the audience
that isn't there.

I will sing and dance, therefore
for the holy one.

Don't Turn Away

Don't turn away
as you tend to do
Listen to what I
have to say

It won't take but
a minute of
your precious time

Look me in the eye and
if you have ears
then hear—the moment
of truth

Say it out loud
your sin—say it
not your little sins
but THE sin

The one that keeps
you from being
what you were meant
to be in this world

Yell it out; confess!
It's already written
down in the book
don't act surprised at that

Just let it lie on the floor
of your folly and
dance with the Lord
of the universe

as you are set free
free as the lioness
the sea turtle
the great gray heron

Fly if you can
but if not – just
rest and breathe
the cool clear air
of forgiveness

I am drunk

With redemption's sacred suds
I weave, stammer, & lean
Against a wall appalled
As I stare into this
Bourbon and water wonder glass
Of grace

There are no more laws
Just swing open the door to the
Saloon and yell: all you drunkards are
Loved by God, so start
Breaking up the place!

The only ones who can
Join in this Holy brawl
Are those who believe
The bar stays open 24-7
And on into eternity
Where the drinks are free

I heard the wine and milk are good

I'm always thinking about God

I can't tell you why
Can't see a spirit is why I may
think so much about it
or to make God stand out
in the crowded forest world
come out of the shadows

When I turned 33 as old as
Jesus I thought I have done
nothing and Jesus has gone
and saved the whole damned
world from hell
only it doesn't look that way

reading the newspaper
about all the murdering and raping
guys taking meat cleavers
to school kids over there in China
and the so-called men of God
abusing innocent little ones
and I've got to wonder

what the hell is going on
So I think about all that
and say: there has got to be a hell
don't you think
or does all that awful stuff
just drift away like so much
cottonwood fluff

But I see love, too—lots of it and it
touches me to see a dad
taking a walk with
his little daughter

and how he looks at her
his smile and how she
skips along all happy

No one knows
and I am no more able
to see clearly through the dark
clouds to where
the sun warms
the heavenly sky

In Those Days

In those days the Lord
hardly ever spoke directly
to people, and he did not
appear to them in dreams
very often. 1 Samuel 3:2

In these days God hardly
speaks to anyone directly either
or if he does
is anyone
listening?

Though, once when I was nine or so
my dad and I drove back
from a fishing trip
as the sun sank behind us
and I, filled with a sudden and grateful love
for everything,

Looked up into the sky and silently said
'I love you God'
and God answered with a
shooting star that sliced the heavens

Under such gray skies of these days
and being of a more sober disposition
I rarely look up

No Rules

Put your life
in God's hands
walk forward
         listen
                    love

there are no rules
no, none, never not one
you can't mean that, teacher
yes, none I declare

eat an apple—digest it
gone—you live the apple life
no apple eaten—same thing
no never no rules

but, teacher, the law, torah,
eightfold path…ah…
none I say—hold up your hand
count your fingers—see light
shine through them—they
are shadow

light is real—shut your eyes
no more light
gone never no more rules
god is love—count love
on your fingers behind
your eyes

lay down on a bridge
wait for the water to rise
sweep you away
where trees grow tall
wind sets you free

Prayers

A runner prays, "Let all success be mine."
Her rival prays, "I want to win this time."

A slave prays, "Lord, please set me free today."
His master prays: "Don't let him run away."

One soldier prays, "Let bullets pass me by."
His foeman prays, "Give me a marksman's eye."

The lover: "Keep her always true to me."
His beloved: "Hide my infidelity."

The son prays, "May my father wake and rise."
His daughter prays, "I hope my father dies."

How God answers each prayer, I cannot say;
Just give me heaven's wisdom when I pray.

The Labyrinth

The object is not
to find the center
just walk slowly
on this broad earth
the seasons are bridges
      gaze at the path below
      up at the shingle sky
gaze inward
    feel the
    heartbeat
        of God

This is a confession where

I stumble into a cathedral
make my way along the marble floor
I want forgiveness
for the way I've acted

I scoop holy water into my mouth
kneel and genuflect or should I sprinkle
my head and anoint myself with oil
God only knows

It is such humiliation
I suck in my breath
and wander through
nebulous fortifications
sink into a pew

Parchment paper scroll
on it is written my sins
it is a very long scroll that
includes sexual sins mostly
but also some hateful judgments
toward a couple of bastards
in my third grade class
in Albany Oregon

A town with its own sin
smelling like a giant fart across I-5
and I am glad I did not
have to repent of that stench
just some CEO who never
gave a crap about people downwind
Nutritious breakfast

of banana on my cereal
with some nuts added seems
proof enough I am not
as sinful as I had imagined

Now alone with my thoughts
I shiver for no reason and next
descend into a murky pool
of water into which
I baptize the remainder
of my sinful body

A Chance of Rain

A Chance of Rain
For Diversity Month, March 2003

1.
The car radio announces a chance of rain
(it's Seattle and no one is surprised)
it's a steady gray rain
the kind we're used to
mothers maneuver their minivans
like ferry boats to muddy soccer fields
some moms huddle under umbrellas
swapping stories
wide-hipped mothers surrounded by happy children
cheer and pull at their soggy sweatshirts
that stick to their shoulders

2.
Rain falls on the just and the unjust
that is, rain falls
on the just, who are also unjust,
and on the unjust, who are also just

Under a dark sky, rain descends
on synagogues, mosques, and Methodist churches
new-age dancers in the forest
find shelter under a sprawling cedar
bald headed atheists baptized by the downpour,
run from their hybrids to discuss
the rise and fall of intolerance
and the lies we tell ourselves
about equality, privilege, and power

3.

The pretty blond weathergirl predicts
we'll look away from:
he motorized wheelchairs of the quadriplegics
the lunch pails of the mentally impaired
Rain soaks the oval track of the Special Olympics
the athletes, drenched though and through,
keep on laughing

raindrops dance (without a grudge)
on the swimming pools of the rich
they dribble (without compassion)
off the hats of the poor
soaking the mucky ground they work

4.

The wild wet weather does not stop peace marchers
from singing songs to protest the rain that
mingles with the blood of the fallen
mingles with the blood of children
(called collateral damage)
paint runs down signs that declare: NO MORE WAR!
generals wring their sweaty hands over tactical maps

It rains on the picnics of those
who recoil from consuming meat;
it rains on the picnics of those who slather
mr. parker's barbeque sauce on a rack of ribs
sizzling over hot coals

5.
Rain washes the gnarled hands
of the old man grasping his walker
it rains regrets for his weakened limbs,
failing eyesight
leaves his hopes sopping wet at his feet
a fine mist conceals death
waiting to pounce

Up north in Skagit Valley, the tulip fields
form a tapestry of vivid colors
becoming a metaphor for you and me walking
this wide wet earth

after a rainstorm small children
prance in new brown puddles
and some, who hate to get their feet wet
look up to the sky for the sun
and the promised
rainbow

Anatomy Lab

I (foolishly or not)
offered my body to our local
medical school to be studied
            after I die.

as is customary, my gray remains will
be subjected to a rude intrusion,
my skull sawed in half to

show off my medulla oblongata
and no amount of luck would
cause me to stand up and say, "Stop it!"

so, for the benefit of some eager
pre-med students, they will gently
tear me apart; study
my muscles and bones,
dissect my eyeballs, and
decipher my stringy nerves.

all through the night I will lie and wait
under a damp sheet for daybreak to bring
the cold steel, and prying fingers that will
lay waste to what I cherish;
what I call 'myself.'

Life and Death

Power-walking on my way
Jogging, stretching, bending
Eating wisely everyday
Keep my life from ending

Sipping coffee all alone
Writing in my journal
I'll eat a whole wheat scone and
Ponder life eternal

Like a grape upon a vine
Waiting for the squeezing
Clutching what I think is mine
Hope I don't die freezing

Like an apple on a tree
I hang beneath the sky
Wonder: Is this all I'll be
Or end up in your pie?

All this worry over life
And death is sad you see
All this anguish, pain, and strife
Will be the death of me

Small Vinyl Box

My mother's ashes poured
Into a small black vinyl box
(Her chemical self) is what
I carry down the freeway
Early on a Monday morning
To the cemetery for burial
With rain pelting my windshield
Rain—just like the day
She bore, named, and held me
Close to her breast

This cycle of birth and death
Causes me to reflect
On how a life gets compressed into
A 10 by 8 by 6-inch box
I give to an old bearded caretaker
Who promises he will
Give it a proper burial
After he finishes
Fixing the brakes
On his '82 Chevy pickup

Street Wait

1.
Outside the tattoo
shop he stands
his body
a canvass
rainbow arms
cell phone and cigarette
checks it and waits
checks it and waits

2.
Along the avenue
homeless
gather
bum cigarettes
by the city shelter
line up to nowhere
check the garbage
smoke
flick ashes
dropped like seeds
sowing
    nothing

The March

The rattle of the snare
rip, rip, of trumpets
parade
no one leads
no one follows
we just march
sing out of tune

turn our faces to the side where
spectators sneer—this
makes us tremble
stumble
the ground is rough
muddy water
into the night

some are lost
some made stronger
some forgive, forget
those who are angered, wait

when my turn
comes
I write a mythology
of mud and disaster
of finding one's way
even in darkness

The water rises

Wiping away the boats, the dock,
The town, the hills behind the town

The highlands are no refuge
The hills no answer
The treetops laugh as I climb

The water rises
Wiping away the boats, the dock,
The town, the hills behind the town
Adrift

The shore
The shore shifts
The center of the world shifts
The town, the hills behind the town
The boats and dock shift

The water rises
The center of the world moves
Wiping away the boats, the dock
The town, the hills behind the town

Everything adrift

Tomorrow and tomorrow

And all the tomorrows as far as the soul can see
And on into eternity
This starts immediately

And there is a bridge across
A great expanse, a chasm
This bridge is a long one
And you can run for days and not reach the other side

And don't look down
You could fall or faint
Look instead beyond
Look inward
Look deep into the eyes of your knowing soul
Look with new eyes, with soulful eyes

And those who turn back
Or look down
Or refuse to keep on running
Will stumble or tumble

Those who press on into
Those vast tomorrows
And on into eternity
Will reap a great reward

The chasm is deep
The bridge is narrow
But the soul is buoyant
So you fly
No bridge is needed

Out There

You are out there somewhere
not the one I should have married
not even close to her—you're the one
adrift in the middle of a crowd
and you taunt me while I sleep

a cold breeze scours your
hot skin; you shiver
powdery snow drifts around
my lips grow frosty
my moustache ices over

I can't see you but
I feel you through my skin
into the bone of my dry bone
and it isn't love, lust
or even luck

you are near—perhaps you float
above us in the cool blue
arms out, back arched
searching the earth

I hope you won't find me
you'd burn me with your eyes
breathe me in—
bury me under your whispers
and your long flat braids

SACKCLOTH AND ASHES

Sackcloth and Ashes

None of us tears our garments any more
when our sins weigh us down
or we are sick with sorrow
like those bible kings of old

They'd rip their clothes
pour ashes on their sorry heads
to let their shame or sadness show

That time I shook my teenage son too hard
when he refused to mow the lawn
might've called for that

It would've done me and him some good
if I'd ripped my tee shirt and jeans
dumped some fireplace
ashes in my hair;
then gone and knocked on his bedroom door
and said I'd been wrong

We could've laughed together
but instead I lay awake
thinking about my misplaced rage
how I waited until he'd grown
into a man to humbly ask
him to forgive me

Travels

I pluck blackbirds from the telephone wires
and put them in a paper bag   my basement
is full of them
and all of this is weighing me down

I've been from Dowddelyn
to Beijing and from Lisbon
to Hana, Hawaii   and never once
spoke the language or killed anything but cockroaches

I'm a tourist of your eyebrows
the faint mustache above your pretty lips
the shores of sorrow   and back again   blinded by
duty   I pass a sentinel standing guard
over mercy and grace

In the years of years a single tear
announces a blue avenue down my leg
where little dams have stopped the flow of blood
I look homeward   walking with measured steps
          calculating the distance

I landed in Paris and never stayed   mercy
how fast my plane can fly   my words float
back across the ocean   breakfast in Amsterdam
toast in London with a long drink of warm beer

It never got cold enough to winterize   moss grows
on my roof until I poison it   when I leave for work
the roads are full   the last moon-smile is fading
I approach an intersection
          where lies and promises
                    collide

She is nothing to me

just a head
in the Metro bus window
speeding by

she'll stick with me though
melt like sugar crystals
in the milky membranes
of my memory banks

not even a glance my way
her cell phone glued to her ear
perched as I am
on the lips of dawn
the sidewalk a parapet

my lazy eye
cocks like a gun
snaps the shot
tight curls, a tangle really
she doesn't need a comb
(this is just an hypothesis)

but on her earlobe
flashes my life story
told in bold fonts

perfume? I don't know
the bus exhaust and all

is her nose pierced?
if so—I'll be so glad

Fire Breathing Egg

If I ask for an egg will
You give me last year's calendar
A hula hoop?

If I ask for a kiss
Will you drink my hot blood
Cold-hearted as you are
With your deep
Ocean eyes?

Can I count on you
To pass the salt
Would you turn me into a pillar
If I happen look back?
Or cast your spell and turn me

Into a fire breathing egg, or
Throw me hard fast
Into the dungeon onion
Breath of your love.

Retirement

The yawning years
Means shifting gears
I take my time
To write this rhyme

The memories
The reveries
The shirtfront soiled
The grandkids spoiled

My shoulder aches
My ankle shakes
I exercise
To stay alive

Scrap books filled
My teeth all drilled
The kids all grown
We're all alone

The phone will ring
Can't hear a thing
I cup my ear
When you are near

The bills are paid
The beds are made
The work is done
It's kinda fun

Time to ponder
Time to wonder
What will happen
After nappin'

antiques

old cedar board smell
garbled vinyl record sound
grandfather's tickless watch
and then
>   a weathered photo
>   brick school house
>   a group of children
>   pose with their teacher
back row
>   my
frowning face

Broken Shells

Shells broken
Scattered across the beach scattered
Wind blows back my parka hood
Revealing
My tear-filled eyes

how a boy goes

how a boy goes where he is not supposed to go into the "off-limits" places
like the garbage dump behind the trailer park in the heat of an afternoon
to look for those discarded treasures, tossed from boxes and bags down
this hillside of refuse, quite colorful, complex bits and pieces of
things a boy finds of great interest and of some use to keep or
for trading and how he trips and tumbles forward his hand
slides hard onto the broken jar and how it slices
into his flesh so the blood flows profusely
the gaping wound worries him, terrifies
because it came from the forbidden
place and he will tell just how it
happened (because he doesn't
think of telling lies yet) and
shaming words will pour
down on him and how
the pain of the body
can't match the
pain of shame
soul pain

So, it has come to this...

I am looking for my socks
While dressing in the local gym
And I find them on my feet

I know I shouldn't complain
You want to chide me saying
I should be glad I have feet
(There are people without legs)

And I would say back
You should be glad
You have a mouth
To say such insolent things
(Some people do not have heads)

And furthermore
It is only by the grace of God
That I put you in my poem, anyway

And I am glad I have eyes
To find my socks on my feet
And to lay in my hammock
On this warm summer day
Watching the clouds
Frolic in the heavens above
With the help of
Avogadro's Law of Gases

Earth Cottage

Earth Cottage

Since the earth is our home
and we all live here
we need to share
the bathroom and

the towels. We all look out
at the same universe of stars;
the same moon, we
all breathe
the same air.

Can we meet tonight
in the living room and
have a little talk about
who left the cap off
the toothpaste? Why there
is no peace.

The boys are fighting
on the front porch, Mama
just slapped Bobbie again
and Juan stabbed Uncle Chang
with the butter knife. What on earth
is going on here? What
will the neighbors think?

Mop up the blood,
Put the kettle on for tea,
Aunt Mobisha will be here
any minute

talk to me about the moon

the one that follows my car
poking its face between trees and hills
as I speed wishful or afraid

the one that trails through dark heavens
as slow as a watch hand
making its way without a care

talk to me about the moon
with its wide gray eyes;
twisted smile as I walk through
the doorway to inhabit my life

talk to me about the moon
as it sinks in the morning
hours—its light now dimly
sliding across our bed

the one that gives itself to
rules of pulling tides
making me wallow in moodiness

the one that's only a whisker
of light—a tiny sliver of itself
but just enough to talk about

so talk to me about the moon
talk to me
talk

Together

1. Together
On the ridges above the city
The lights flutter like flowers against the night sky
Starlings have darted away, the night belongs to itself

We are walking along the river bank
As darkness closes in and your hand is cold

That was the night we stood and cried
Holding each against the chill
We gripped, one more time
 the warmth of our understanding

2. Past
There was a time long ago when
We bent like green branches
Took baths together, rubbed our backs

Back then the roads were narrow
Our thumbs were flags to drivers
Who were eager to erase their loneliness
We had nowhere to go except toward
our lightheartedness

3. Question
Why now do we weep? Who's been dead so long?
Why do neighbors turn their backs
Why do little children run away?
Gifts cost too much and our mood is salty, rancid.

Who paints the iron gates and oils the locks?
Whose freedom was stolen
so we're chained together?
Who gave no bread to the poor
leaving them destitute?

4. Blessing

Bless the bus drivers and hillbillies who crowd the city.
Bless those whose bones never grew.
Bless the monks who kept the temple fit for God.

Bless us, who stand in the darkness holding hands.
Bless the river of our baptism.
Bless the light on the ridges above our city

Forest Preacher

As I walk early this morning
the high half-moon
nibbles away at the few remaining stars
or is it the other way around?

A Steller's jay preaches a raucous sermon
of heavenly promises
for those who repent and
turn from unnatural desires

The dark trees raise their lacy hands
to signal their conversion

The leaf-strewn serpentine trail
twists away and I follow
suddenly aware of my hands
pushing deep into my jacket pockets.

Peace One Day

Peach on earth to everyone
who pleases God!
          —the angels in Luke

There will be peace one day
when we get around to pleasing God
and it's a simple thing:
as the bible says: *the only thing*
that matters is love working through you

But oh, the loving—how it leaves us
wondering…
          we wrestle with angels over it
          tear our enemies limb to limb
                    to please our god

Angels still point the way
if we'll become silent
enough to hear them

Try it on a cool, clear night
when the stars burn
 step out alone
and listen
listen…

Sampson

Sampson was a sucker for the girls
Just to touch their soft brown skin he
Traded answers to riddles and secrets of his strength
Ripped the clothes off the backs of thirty men

He was the first blind suicide terrorist
Eye for an eye, exploding a stone roof
Down on men, women, and children
Who simply gathered to celebrate

God gave him the strength to do that
And I wade through the rubble of my misunderstanding
Brush temple dust from my clothes
     Stumble back into this time
     Where I've scheduled my morning
     Workout in a local health club

Silence of the Swallows

The shatter of glass beneath a bulldozer
Clearing the ghetto high-rises is not
A noise of this earth's making

But the glacier's crack and groan
Are of the earth's own tongue
The guttural sounds of high pressure
Slow slip and slide—surface to surface

The roar of the wind
Battle of thunder
Sheeting rain that froths the ocean, yes!

The bang and rattle
The ping, ping of the slot machine
Is from the place newly
Bolted into the human psyche
Not from the earth-child's heart

The sea moves and rages
The sound richly brave
Momentous, catastrophic over eons
But the rip, rip, and whine of
The dirty Chevrolet that grunts
In the morning cold
What is that? It comes from the grave
Of necessity

Listen in the wooded canyon
The whispers across the wilderness lake
Sound of wind through leaves
Listen from the gut of your soul
For the silence of the swallows

Savannah's Hydrangeas

Savannah needs her hydrangeas
replanted—I'm glad to do it.
She can't because
a disease causes her skin to
bind her like a mummy.
It's okay to cry out my eyes.

This winter I wanted
to sit by my fire and read,
but instead I've been called
to a distant land.
I'll be uprooted
like Savannah's hydrangeas, so
I've been dragging my feet
like a three-year-old at the barber:
 "I won't cut off your head, little guy."
"Right," I say.

On my morning walk,
instead of the paved path
I take the muddy horse trail.
"I don't call you to the safe, dry life,"
God whispers, while
I cry out my eyes—
but the message is clear.

What happens on the inside
is what counts
the outside world spins
like a dervish without
rhythm or soothing drums.
It's the whoosh and roar
of the jetliner taking me
away from my fire and hearth;
far from Savannah's hydrangeas.

Wars and Rumors

What with war—
War talk, we wonder
Is the Prince of Peace,
Born long ago
            still here?

Is He still
Saving us
With his
            birth-death?

Will we, whom he saves,
Spread kindness like soft butter
On the wounded
            bread
            of this life?

Could we close our eyes
And make
            a foolish wish?
Wishing:
When we
Open them we'll see
The Prince of Peace pour
a healing balm
            upon this tortured earth

TIME

Time...

to get up
and stick my tongue
on the frozen pole
of a new day.

I Am Who I Am

From the flaming desert bush
God spoke, "I am who I am."
I echo back, "I am who I am."
The red sun circles the earth

Out of my womb cave
I answer a call from distant hills
Venturing out into the heat
I trudge a life

In this desert
Sand dunes rise and fall
Palm trees sit beside still waters
Dusk brings a chill

My lonely eyes
Scan the muted desert miles
I gather sticks for a fire
Make my bed with solitude

Winds whistle across the expanse
I lie back on the soft earth
Breathe in the gift of night fragrances
Search the sky for the first evening star

There is no horizon at night
But stars dance in a friendly sky
A dream camel pads over this ancient ocean bottom
A cry from its rider pierces my silence:
"You are who you are."

Another Day

The red morning
Pierces your sleepy eye, Ms. Bradley
It's the edge of another day

Your breath floats in and out
You drift to the kitchen, light up,
Toast some bread, heat coffee

You get nailed to the couch by sitcoms
Where laughter rises and falls
With the slide of a technician's switch

Your hungry life might get better
If you'd quit smoking, find a friend
Lose some weight, make luscious love again

The night job at Lucky's Market
Like a mild drug, brings relief: the beer guy
Tells his jokes, a new People magazine arrives

Ms. Bradley, I want to call and tell you that
You're afraid to lose, afraid to win
Afraid to fall, afraid to soar above
Your puzzle-life with its pieces strewn about
but I don't know your number

The evening sun turns red, worn sheets
Beckon you to dream things are different
Which of course they are not

Your phone rings
But you won't pick it up

Lord Sun Visits Seattle

In the heavens a tent
is set up for the sun.
It rises like a bridegroom
and gets ready like a hero
eager to run a race.
It travels all the way
across the sky.
Nothing hides from its heat
—Ps 19:4-6

In this rain-drenched place
the sun is a shy god
who burns behind
his shield of clouds

so when he does appear
we're shocked worshippers
who run out and smile
bare our lucky arms

the red leaves glow
in praise of such a one
who sings in the shower
but seldom on the stage

yet if he shines
for just a single hour
my wife runs out to garden
her white hair ablaze

my late afternoon sandwich
is a Eucharist of sorts

with cheese and mayo
chopped golden pepperoncini

soon Lord Sun hides behind
cottonwood tree curtains
slinks slowly out of sight
without even taking a bow

she thought she heard

angels breathe
soft as desert sand
wind that gently stirred the leaves

beneath her feet—solid earth
above—the firmament
all was still
as a country wheat field
on a summer evening

then—their breathing
   she thought she heard
     she wept
not despair
but something
like a child's arms
reaching for a mother

so she breathed
with them in unison
knew how small she was
how far from home

That spring...

I stopped listening to my heart
Did not enjoy the glint of frost
On the branch—I simply folded in on myself

This lack of mindfulness puzzled me
Until I realized I had been thinking
About the peacemaker Tom Fox
Who was tortured and killed in Iraq that week

No, I hadn't noticed the robins had
Picked the holly tree clean of berries
My wife needed to tell me that

I simply had to wait for the grace train
And for the conductor to guide me
To the observation deck and point out
The spring colors, the new buds on cherry trees
The tiny ferns breaking ground in the backyard

reservations

even if the
wall of sky
      drops like
      the final curtain
on the Romeo and Juliette
days of my life

even if on odd days
I'm carried down
      the aisle of no intermission
to where dust collects in the
      corners of my backstage
      memories

even (and this is the final) if
the applause
      drowns out
      the front row
      dream of you
and my torn ticket heart
      falls to the sticky floor
      I will
      I will
      continue
to reserve a seat each night
as long as the season lasts

Travels II

It has taken
A lifetime to grow these toenails
That now curl under my gnarled digits
The nights have sped by
       stars a million tiny blurs
       God's creation story
       written on billboards along a
       freeway—cars whizzing by
Mercy has followed me, though
Caught up with me now and again
When I spun out on gravel
Slowed me down
       when I was ditched and in a dither
I swim
       across the rivers of my blood
       pumped clean over & over
       just to get dirty again like
       unruly preschoolers left outside
       after a rainy morning

To tell the truth, I've nowhere
To go
       and ought to stand still;
       let the dust of
       my dreams drift
       on ahead
Magical dust
       of one still wondering

The Night Train

The train you see
Sitting on the tracks
Will leave in twenty minutes
Leave, and not return

You'd better get on board
This is the last train that will take
You where you want to go
Your sleeping coach is ready
Tea is on the table

When this train leaves the station
It won't be coming back
Once it's gone
It's gone—gone

Don't be afraid to climb on board
This is a one-way ride
But it is the only train that will
Take you where you want to go
It won't be coming back

The covers are turned down
A mint is on your pillow
It is the night train
But morning will be its destination
Morning

Look in the windows
Shadowy figures move about
A small girl waves from a door well
To no one in particular

Will you step on board?
There are no more trains tonight
Or any other night
This is the only train
That will take you where you want to go

As evening thickens
The train will be well on its way
Slip on your nightclothes
The steward will tuck you in
Give you small gifts of eyeshades
Toothbrush, mouth rinse

Turn your face to the wall
You'll drowse and roll
With the sway of your coach
The click-clicking wheels
Of the night train
That will not be coming back

The night train that will
Take you where you want to go

AUTHOR

Jim Teeters has published poetry and articles in *Spirituality and Health, Hiram Poetry Review, Beginnings,* and *Friends Church* publications. He is the author of *Teach with Style: A Comprehensive System for Teaching Adults* (Redleaf Press) and *Going Intergenerational: All Ages Learning Bible Truths Together* (Barclay Press). He has spent many years working with people through teaching and training, Friends Church ministries, and social services. Jim is a retired social worker from Kent, Washington but still conducts training through Adults Teaching Adults. Jim lives in Kent, Washington with his wife, Rebecca. *Don't Turn Away* is his forth collection of poetry. His email: jim.ata@comcast.net.

Made in the USA
Charleston, SC
09 March 2011